URANUS

by L. L. Owens

Published by The Child's World®
1980 Lookout Drive • Mankato, MN 56003-1705
800-599-READ • www.childsworld.com

ACKNOWLEDGMENTS
The Child's World®: Mary Berendes, Publishing Director
The Design Lab: Design and production
Red Line Editorial: Editorial direction

PHOTO CREDITS
NASA/courtesy of nasaimages.org, cover, 1, 3, 6, 8, 12, 14, 16, 17, 19, 21,
23, 27, 29, 31, 32; Heidi Hammel (Massachusetts Institute of Technology)
and NASA/courtesy of nasaimages.org, 5; NASA/courtesy of nasaimages.
org/The Design Lab, 6, 7, 9; NASA/NSSDC/EIT Consortium, 11; NASA/
NSSDC/Catalog of Spaceborne Imaging, 13; AP Images/North Wind Picture
Archives, 15; NASA, ESA, L. Sromovsky and P. Fry (University of Wisconsin-
Madison), H. Hammel (Space Science Institute), and K. Rages (SETI Institute)/
courtesy of nasaimages.org, 25

LIBRARY OF CONGRESS CATALOGING-IN-PUBLICATION DATA
Owens, L. L.
  Uranus / by L.L. Owens.
    p. cm.
  Includes bibliographical references and index.
  ISBN 978-1-60954-389-1 (library bound : alk. paper)
  1. Uranus (Planet)—Juvenile literature. I. Title.
  QB681.O94 2010
  523.47—dc22

                          2010040463

Printed in the United States of America
Mankato, MN
December, 2010
PA02072

ON THE COVER
Uranus is known for its
blue-green appearance.

Table of Contents

Uranus and the Solar System

Look through a **telescope** on a starry night. Can you find a blue-green dot of light? It might be the planet Uranus (YOOR-uh-nuss)!

Uranus is one of our space neighbors in the **solar system**. At the center of our solar system is the sun. Planets **orbit**, or go around, the sun.

The colors in this image of Uranus show what a person near the planet might see.

SUN

Mercury
Venus
Earth
Mars
Ceres
Jupiter

Fun Facts

PLANET NUMBER: Uranus is the
seventh planet from the sun.

DISTANCE FROM SUN: 1.78 billion miles
(2.9 billion km)

SIZE: Uranus is about 99,787 miles
(160,592 km) around its middle. That's about
four times bigger than Earth's middle.

OUR SOLAR SYSTEM: Our solar system has eight
planets and five dwarf planets. Pluto used to be
called a planet. But in 2006, scientists decided to call it a
dwarf planet instead. Scientists hope to discover even more
dwarf planets in our solar system!

Saturn

Uranus

Neptune

Pluto

Haumea

Makemake

Eris

- Planet
- Dwarf Planet

While orbiting the sun, a planet spins, or rotates, on its **axis**. An axis is an imaginary line that runs through the planet. Most planets have an axis that runs from top to bottom. But Uranus is tipped almost completely sideways. Its rotation looks more like rolling than spinning.

One full spin on the axis equals one day— the time from one sunrise to the next sunrise. A day on Earth is 24 hours. Uranus rotates once every 17 hours.

An axis runs through the center of a planet. The planet spins on the axis.

One year is the time it takes for a planet to travel once around the sun. A year on Earth is about 365 days. But it takes Uranus about 30,685 days to go around the sun—that's about 84 Earth years!

The sun is a star at the center of our solar system. Uranus takes a long time to go around the sun.

A Gas Giant

Uranus is a kind of planet called a **gas** giant. It is made of layers of gas and liquid. Other planets have hard, rocky surfaces with mountains and volcanoes.

Fun Fact

There are two types of planets.

TERRESTRIAL PLANETS (mostly rock) are close to the sun. They are: Mercury, Venus, Earth, and Mars.

GAS GIANTS (mostly gas and liquid) are farther from the sun. They are: Jupiter, Saturn, Uranus, and Neptune.

Some of Uranus's layers of
gas look hazy.

A New Discovery

In 1781, William Herschel studied the night sky from England. He saw a curious glowing disk through his homemade telescope. It was blue and a little fuzzy.

His sister Caroline looked, too. They realized that William had found a new planet—the seventh! Uranus was named after the Greek god of the heavens.

Fun Fact

People have observed the first six planets for thousands of years. Those planets are easy to see without a telescope.

William Herschel and his
sister Caroline saw Uranus
through a telescope.

The View from Space

Uranus is far from Earth—about 1.6 billion miles (2.6 billion km). That makes it difficult to study. For 200 years, scientists hoped to someday get close enough to see it better.

NASA's spacecraft *Voyager 2* finally flew by Uranus in 1986. The spacecraft took thousands of pictures of the mysterious planet.

Fun Fact

NASA stands for the National Aeronautics and Space Administration. It is a US agency that studies space and the planets.

The *Voyager 2* spacecraft was launched in 1977.

TITAN/CENTAUR COMPLEX 41

Other tools gather **data** about Uranus, too. In 1994, the Hubble Space Telescope's powerful cameras showed us some of Uranus's rings, moons, and bright clouds.

In 2009, scientists counted 13 thin, icy rings around Uranus. Twenty-seven moons orbit the planet.

This image from *Voyager 2* shows nine rings around Uranus.

19

Conditions on Uranus

Uranus's sideways spin affects conditions there. During half the orbit, the planet's north pole faces the sun, and the south pole is swallowed in complete darkness. Then they switch. One season of darkness on a Uranus pole lasts half a human's lifetime! Can you imagine living 42 years without seeing the sun?

This image shows Uranus,
its rings, and some of
its moons.

At all times, Uranus is very cold. The temperature is usually about −357°F (−216°C). On Earth, water turns to ice at 32°F (0°C).

A planet's **atmosphere** is the layer of gas around it. Earth's atmosphere is the air we breathe. The thick atmosphere on Uranus looks like blue-green clouds. The cold temperature causes some of the gases to freeze into ice. But this ice is not made from water.

The Hubble Space Telescope orbits Earth. It has taken photos of Uranus that help scientists study the planet.

Scientists used to think weather on Uranus was calm. But new information shows high winds and strong storms. In 2006, scientists spotted a dark cloud. It was a **cyclone**. The storm was big enough to cover most of the United States!

The dark spot shown in the white box is a 2006 storm on Uranus.

Future Exploration

Scientists continue to study Uranus for important clues. They think water is present in the planet's atmosphere. All life as we know it needs water. Searching for water on other planets helps us search for signs of life in other places in our solar system.

Scientists study Uranus's moons, including icy, rocky Miranda.

And what is underneath that atmosphere? Scientists think Uranus could have oceans made of liquid diamonds!

Much of what happens on the planet is still a mystery. But scientists are excited to see what Uranus could teach us!

Scientists continue to study
the hazy, blue-green
planet Uranus.

GLOSSARY

atmosphere (AT-muhss-fihr): An atmosphere is the mixture of gases around a planet or a star. Uranus has a thick atmosphere.

axis (AK-siss): An axis is an imaginary line that runs through the center of a planet or a moon. Uranus rotates on its axis.

cyclone (SYE-klone): A cyclone is a tornado, or a swirling storm with high winds that looks like a funnel. In 2006, scientists saw a cyclone on Uranus.

data (DAY-tuh): Data are facts, figures, and other information. Scientists hope to learn more data about Uranus.

dwarf planets (DWORF PLAN-itz): Dwarf planets are round bodies in space that orbit the sun, are not moons, and are not large enough to clear away their paths around the sun. Dwarf planets often have similar objects that orbit near them.

gas (GASS): A gas is a substance that moves around freely and can spread out. Uranus is a planet made of layers of gas.

observed (uhb-ZURVD): If something is observed, it is watched and studied closely. People who lived thousands of years ago observed the first six planets, but Uranus was not discovered until 1781.

orbit (OR-bit): To orbit is to travel around another body in space, often in an oval path. Planets orbit the sun.

solar system (SOH-lur SISS-tum): Our solar system is made up of the sun, eight planets and their moons, and smaller bodies that orbit the sun. Uranus is the seventh planet from the sun in our solar system.

telescope (TEL-uh-skope): A telescope is a tool that makes faraway objects look closer. William Herschel discovered Uranus using a homemade telescope.

FURTHER INFORMATION

BOOKS

Landau, Elaine. *Uranus*. New York: Children's Press, 2008.

Stewart, Melissa. *Uranus*. New York: Franklin Watts, 2002.

Trammel, Howard K. *The Solar System*. New York: Children's Press, 2010.

WEB SITES

Visit our Web site for links about Uranus: **childsworld.com/links**

Note to Parents, Teachers, and Librarians: We routinely verify our Web links to make sure they are safe and active sites. So encourage your readers to check them out!

INDEX

ABOUT THE AUTHOR

L. L. Owens has been writing books for children since 1998. She writes both fiction and nonfiction and especially loves helping kids explore the world around them.